ONE-MINUTE MY~ ~~ ~~

Simon Parke has worked for Sainsbury's,
Spitting Image *and the Church of England. He has also
Paused for Thought with Terry Wogan, run the
London Marathon and written three novels:*
Desert Depths, Desert Ascent *and* Desert Child.
*He is married with two children and lives
in North London.*

Dedicated to the Dove who breaks the circle, and helps me breathe again

ONE-MINUTE MYSTIC

For Those with only 59 Seconds to Spare

SIMON PARKE

First published in Great Britain in 1999
Azure Books
1 Marylebone Road
London NW1 4DU

Copyright © Simon Parke 1999

British Library Cataloguing-in-Publication Data

A catalogue record for this book is available from the British Library

ISBN 1-902694-00-7

Typeset in Benguiat by
Pioneer Associates, Perthshire
Printed in Malta by
Interprint Limited

INTRODUCTION

Some people think that mysticism takes, if not an eternity, at least a lifetime. They also think to be a mystic means wearing a pointy hat and a long robe, living alone on a hill East of Nowhere (or South Kensington) having given up *everything*, in dedicated pursuit of becoming a crank. None of this is true. Or to put it another way, all of this is false. To become a mystic you can remain where you are and carry on doing what you're doing; clothes are up to you but what you're wearing now looks fine. And it doesn't take a lifetime. Indeed, it can take as little as a minute. Or less. Which is just as well, really, because some of us have only 59 seconds to spare . . .

Now obviously any book about mysticism worth its nuts is going to be concerned largely with God, pain, sex, friendship, reality and the learning of love. This book is. So if none of these topics interest you, read no further. (Though you may want to go to see your doctor to check that you're still alive.) But no – if you're cosy in your little corner, happy with your blinkers, and content with the thin slice of reality you feed off, good luck and good hunting. But goodbye. The paths separate here.

The rest of us, however, need to be wary too. For the mystic river we now find ourselves walking beside is a dangerous piece of water. I'd be less than a good guide if I didn't mention that. Mysticism has seduced the vulnerable, destroyed the unstable and broken the so-called strong. To change the metaphor, mysticism is a relentless hunter of all those on the run from reality, which is certainly me and may occasionally be you. It will require everything of you. But prove to be all gift.

So a short pause by the water is appropriate. Before we jump in. Or before we even dip our toe in the shallow lapping water at the edge. And in that pause, we might ask ourselves a question, because questions are much more adult than answers, and the question is this: what do I want? What, in the deepest place within me, do I desire? Don't worry if you don't know the answer. It's a surprisingly hard one. But would you at least like to find out?

Someone said you might as well try and pin down smoke as describe mysticism. And certainly these pages are not concerned with telling you what to believe. You're grown up now. You can decide that for yourself. But mysticism *can* be described, can be defined and will be. What mysticism can't be, however, is *organized*. Like all adventures, it is not only dangerous – it's unpredictable. I can describe the lion. But I can't tell you when it will strike. But you will know when it does. And surprisingly, you will recognize the moment more in its joy than in its pain.

In the meantime, I will be a friend of sorts to you, willing you on, willing you to hang in there, for my eyes cry for you as well as for myself. But ultimately the journey is yours, for no one else can tend your soul: the eternal soul within you, the soul which is so close to so much. So close to loving, so close to feeling, so close to lying, so close to dying, so close to anger, so close to seeing, so close to happy, so close to sad, so close to neighbour, so close to God.

These are the days of our lives. Starting now.

⟪ SAFETY FIRST ⟫

Everyone was very critical of the school. It was *terrible*.
But the Muslim child who was showing me around
spoke warmly of it, and it soon became obvious why.
He felt safe there. Secure. Whatever else the school
could or couldn't offer, it had given him the greatest
gift for growth, for adventure – a deep sense of safety.

I think what I'm trying to ask you is whether you feel
loved? Have you ever felt loved? It makes a difference.
It makes a difference to what is possible in your
life, possible today . . .

THE HARDEST THING ON EARTH

Some people say a diamond is the hardest thing on earth.
I don't think so. I think the hardest thing on earth is to
stand in someone else's shoes, enter into someone
else's world. To feel the feelings of a mother losing a
child at 22 weeks; to know how a flower experiences
the gentle rays of the sun; to understand the alienation
of the gaunt-eyed street-hard youth.

So the hardest thing on earth is mysticism. Because
mysticism is the attempt at union with reality.
Mysticism is beginning to live not just
in your little world. But in all the little
worlds around you.

Mysticism is union. Union. Union.

 NORWICH

The city has a football team. It has
a cathedral. It has Alan Partridge.
In 1373, it also had a 30-year-old recluse called Julian:
a woman who (reportedly whilst in bed
and at death's door)
received a series of 16 visions. In 1393, after
20 years' reflection (no rush or anything), she
dared tell us what she thought they might be about.

The Revelations of Divine Love.
And the most famous line from them is this:
'All shall be well, and all shall be well, and
all manner of thing shall be well.'

Imagine it.

 GOSPEL?

The Gospel of Thomas was discovered
in 1945 in the Nag Hammadi desert.
It hadn't made it into the Bible.
But rather, had sat sealed and secret
amidst the dry places of Upper Egypt.

Reportedly, it was dictated by Jesus to his
brother, Judas Thomas the Twin.
Many think it contains original sayings
of Jesus.

This is one of them. Listen.

'When you know yourselves, then you will be
known, and you will understand that you are
children of the living father. But if you do not
know yourselves, then you dwell in poverty,
and you are poverty.'

⤳ CONSEQUENCES ⤵

They say a vision without a task is just a dream.
And a task without a vision just a drudge.
But a task *and* a vision is hope.

If union with reality is the *vision* of mysticism,
then relating to reality is the *task*.
Relating to yourself. (Hard for you or easy?)
Relating to others. (Hard for you or easy?)
Relating to God. (Hard for you or easy?)

Still, the consequence is worth a bob or two.
Hope.
So . . .

 **SEX**

Sex is release, sex is union, sex is passion, sex is desire,
sex is empty, sex is creation, sex is struggle, sex is
disappointment, sex is dangerous, sex is longing,
sex is belonging, sex is distance, sex is penetration,
sex is receiving, sex is failure, sex is bad,
sex is domination, sex is love, sex is submission,
sex is not rational, sex is self-hate, sex is good.

Sex and mysticism are very similar.

 **GOLD**

No one digs two hundred feet deep for gold,
when they know there's gold just five feet from
the surface. What's the point? Life's too short
for that sort of nonsense.

But what about when the gold from the
surface runs out – when you've exhausted it?
And maybe yourself too. *Then* you might think
about the gold two hundred feet deep.

Mysticism is not the calling for those enjoying
the five-feet-deep experience. But for
those for whom easy access to gold has run
out – yet who believe there is more
deeper down, and are prepared for excavation.

 THE TRUTH

If you had to choose between Jesus and the truth, which would you choose?

It would never happen.

I know. But if it did, which would you choose?

It's impossible.

Of course. But just suppose the impossible. Which would you choose?

I'd choose the truth.

Then one day you might be a mystic.

# TRANSFORMATION

Mysticism is not primarily concerned with
fascinating and curious new states of mind.
But rather, with your transformation.

If you have the guts to face the follow-the-crowd spirit
which has you in its grip, and give up the illusion
that you are captain of your soul, then a different
wind will fill your sails.

It's a wind which drove the rich young St Francis
to embrace poverty;
Catherine of Siena into politics; and Florence Nightingale
into confrontation with bureaucrats, scuttling rats,
urine and disease in the military hospitals of
the Crimea.

No wonder God has so few friends.

HOW OFTEN DO YOU DO IT?

Apparently we spend 12 years of our lives
watching telly; two and a half years on the phone;
and have sex 2,500 times. Nice work if you
can get it. But what about praying? How long?
And how often?

Aspiring mystics in the fourth century fled to
the desert to escape the distractions.
But the desert is very expensive these days,
so twentieth-century mystics may need to learn
to pray *during* sex and phone calls and telly.

Then if occasionally you want to go to the
desert as well – or even to a mosque, synagogue
or church – fine. Any place where you find a
soul-opening stillness . . .

MY LIFE BY MR P. STONE

Must be hard being a paving stone,
in a busy street. All those people walking
over you, dropping their junk on you. The chewing gum
must be the worst. The way it sticks and hardens
dirt black. And the cold. And no thanks from anyone.
But then there are the peaceful times, I suppose
when the rush stops. And sometimes
the rain washes, and the sun warms,
and sometimes there's that nice man with
the broom, to scrape away the gum.

All in all, it's a mixed bag being a paving stone.
Like being human. But I'm a better human
for having reflected on Mr Stone. Like me, he's
part of creation and we all need to stick together.

 GRASS

On Monday, the man told me that grass is often green.
I said, how ridiculous, and argued my case rather well.

On Tuesday, the man told me that grass is often green.
I said I had occasionally seen green grass. But not to
the extent that he suggested.

On Wednesday, the man told me that grass is often green.
I can't remember how I replied.

On Thursday, I told the boy that grass is often green.
He said, how ridiculous.
And argued his case rather well. Or so he thought.

We can only receive what we are ready to receive.

 BACK TO EDEN

They ought to be shot. Whoever it was.
Whoever it was who told you that it was
a 'butterfly' and so removed the wonder.
Before that, you'd watched in awe, at the
mad colourful air-held wafer-light dance. Now, you just
said: 'Oh that? That's just a butterfly.'

Seek out those who make history young again.
Who fill you with the smells, memories and hopes
of Eden.

It's the path to heaven.

 THE DOG

So I said to the holy woman,
'How do you spend your day?'
'Training the dog is important,' she replied.
'Dog? What dog? I've never seen a dog
with you.'
'The dog guarding the entrance of my soul.
It is important that it learns a new question.
A question other than: "What's in this for me?"'

Teaching an old dog new tricks.
Mystics love a challenge.

 BLUE SKIES

I don't know where in the world or in what century
you would choose to live, if a time machine
became available.
But it wouldn't be England in the fourteenth century. It was
bleak. Unremittingly bleak. Economic upheaval. Social
unrest. And the Plague. Pray for a quick death.

But out of that century came this invitation, this call:
'Smite upon that thick dark cloud of unknowing with
a sharp dart of longing love – and suddenly it shall part
and disclose the blue.'

Longing love. If it can find blue sky in fourteenth-century
England, it can find it anywhere.

 THE TERRIBLE HEAT

Hear ye, hear ye!
An important 'Not'!

The mystic's life is *not* built around the verb 'to have.' The mystic is someone running *away* from the terrible heat of having. Even if they don't always know what they're running *towards*, they're running *from* that. And it isn't completely stupid. When the fire breaks out in the factory, you leave the building. You don't get caught up in a long debate with the bookkeeper about what exactly awaits you in the car park.

 A QUESTION

Some people think that religious conversions
are all about people finding the answers. But
one of the most famous conversions – that of
St Paul, on the road to Damascus – was in fact
built around a question.
In a vision, Christ asked Paul this:
'Why do you persecute me?'

We persecute out of our own unhappiness.
Who will you persecute today? And why?
Persecution is against union.

(Paul, by the way, from that simple question, went
on to become one of the great Christian mystics.
Hope for us all.)

ONE

Reflections on a pilgrimage to Mecca:

'Love, humility, and true brotherhood
was almost a physical feeling wherever I turned.
All ate as One, slept as One. Everything
about the pilgrimage atmosphere accented
the Oneness of Man under One God.'

God.
Our ground for unity.
Yet also one with a very fine
track record in destroying it;
in setting people at one another's throats
in religious war.

Or is it less about God and more about me?
After all, it is *fun* making demons
out of others. And so undemanding on my own
sick self . . .

CHRIS. CROSS-CHANNEL

His head bobs up and down
on the water's surface.
It's choppy in the English Channel,
but Chris is determined.
Amidst white foam and slapping wave,
his strong arms work the surface of the sea,
strong legs push and propel.
Beneath him, untold unexplored depths of
deep dark water.
And France?
Visible certainly – yet still some way away.

The mystic works the surface too.
Small talk, washing up, train times,
deadlines, children to school, spot the ball.
But the mystic knows also the deep
depths of mystery beneath the surface.
And the Kingdom of God?
Visible, certainly – yet still some way away.

 STARK NAKED

In the end, someone had to say it and
the little boy duly obliged. 'The emperor hasn't
got any clothes on.' Everyone else had been
too wrapped up in the status quo, the way things
are, convention. Couldn't see the wood for the trees,
or in this case, couldn't see the thigh for the lie.

No aspiring mystic will unquestioningly
support any human institution, philosophy
or belief – even if the followers claim God as their
friend. (*Particularly* if the followers claim God
as their friend.)

And why this scepticism?
There's too much crap about frankly. In the little
boy's case, it meant being more in tune with
reality than royalty.

 WHAT TO BRING

You buy a nice bottle of wine and bring it
to the party, with some pride in both your
choice and your generosity. You are not
a little upset when the host takes it, smashes it,
and throws it on the skip outside.
And then has the nerve to say 'Welcome'.
Well! I *mean*!

Don't bring your strengths to the task
of becoming a mystic. You'll find they
get smashed. Just bring your longings.
And however it seems, your host really will
mean 'Welcome'.

 DANGEROUS

Sufis are Muslims who seek a close and personal
experience of God. Some Sufis have gone so far
in emphasizing the union of the soul with
God that they were thought to blasphemously
claim that the soul and God were
identical. Al-Hajjaj was executed in 922 for
crying out in ecstatic union with God:
'I am the truth!'

I did mention that mysticism was dangerous.
I hadn't realized it was *that* dangerous . . .

Meister Eckhart lived millions of years ago
in the thirteenth century in a country miles from
anywhere called Germany. So you wouldn't
be interested in what he has to say.
If you were, you'd discover that there's
something he puts before love.

???

Surely *nothing*'s more important than love?
St Paul famously said that faith, hope and
love were the top three, but that love was
undoubtedly and unquestioningly
Numero Uno, the Big Cheese, the Head
Honcho.

So what precisely does Meister Eckhart put
before love? Tell us, that we might laugh in
his thirteenth-century face!

No. No I won't. After all, I've studied the
art of suspense. You must wait! Till you, er,
turn the page.

So not much suspense there then.

Detachment. That's the answer.
Meister Eckhart puts detachment ahead of love.
Not quite as sexy as 'Love' somehow.
I don't see Hollywood advertising 'One
of the greatest detachment stories of all time.'
I don't hear a lot of pained 'detachment songs'
on my radio. Eckhart's having a laugh, isn't he?

Yet until we are able to detach ourselves
from the tyranny of our roller-coaster emotions
and frenetic thoughts, there isn't really a lot God,
or anyone else,
can do. We're slaves frankly. But if we *were* able to,
then –

Oh no, not *more* suspense! Now we'll never know. Ever.
(*Unless, of course, we look at the next page.*)

THE ART OF SUSPENSE (PART 3)

Detach yourself just for a moment
from the fickle twists of your emotions and thoughts,
your *outer* senses, and you may become aware
of the naked flame of intent flickering amidst
your *inner* soul.
Detachment from the *former* allows for
attachment to the *latter*. And the latter, your soul space,
is the place of change, the place of transformation.

Imagine it. Imagine being led by detachment,
however briefly achieved, to the playground
of God within you. The place where real
love is made, and not the pretend stuff we usually
try and get away with.

 FAMILY PAIN

Family pain is one of the hardest mysticisms
to live. Mysticism is union with reality.
Family pain is a fracture of reality, experienced at close
quarters, and it will hurt the mystic more,
not less. For in opening themselves
to the risk of union, mystics also make themselves
more vulnerable to the agony of
disunion in dislocated relationships.

Ask Jesus.
Feel the bleak crucified scream of the abandoned
son on the cross. Yet they say he still
refused the drugged wine offered him.

Mysticism is a commitment to union – not escape.
And sometimes it's terrible. Drugged or undrugged.

 SMALL IS NOT BEAUTIFUL

Jesus was like a fire –
warming those chilled by their perceived inadequacy.
But we are the small people –
using others only to bolster our inadequate selves.

Jesus lived out of a freedom from fear and anxiety.
But we are the small people –
hopelessly belittled by both.

Jesus had a big heart for his fellow travellers,
particularly those limping on the journey,
unwanted, unhealed, unrated.
But we are the small people –
who like those who like us,
who are like us,
and who one day might return the favour.

A mystic is a small person, who's hoping big,
and prepared to face the cost.

 **OPEN**

Open the curtains to the sunlight,
and feel the playful warmth on your face.
Open the window to the breeze
and feel the fresh and the gentle.

We become that to which we are open.
Nice.

But be careful to what you are open.

Open yourself to your need to control,
and you become to others the breath of Satan.
Open yourself to resentment,
grudge, self-pity, or negativity,
and you become the rotting stench of the living corpse.

Be open. But be careful.

We become that to which we are open.

 DISPOSABLE

It didn't take Meister Eckhart long to
notice that a characteristic of creatures
is that they make something out of something.
A bird, for instance, makes a nest out of all sorts.

It took him slightly longer to notice that
God tends to make something out of *nothing*.
This led him to the following conclusion:
if God is to make anything
in you or with you, you must beforehand
have become nothing.

NB. To become nothing means this:
no possession, no doctrine, no ambition, no attitude
within you, which isn't completely and utterly disposable.

That's nothing. And it's everything.

 SHE'S A BLOND

It's not that she can't enjoy herself.
It's not that she can't laugh.
She can and does with the best of them.
And can she create?!
She creates with paint, clay, cloth and words.

But beneath and within, is a river of pain.
A river of pain runs through her.
Sometimes she pretends it isn't there.
But most of the time she chooses union with this reality.
And in that choosing lies her crucifixion.
And her resurrection.

She's a blond, she's a mystic –
and she lives round the corner.

 SWINK AND SWEAT

In the healing work of psychiatric units all over
the world, lives a crucial commitment:
a commitment to reality.

In the healing work of
psychotherapists all over the world,
lives a crucial commitment:
a commitment to reality.

In *The Cloud of Unknowing*
the work of an anonymous fourteenth-century mystic,
lives a crucial commitment:
a commitment to reality.

In his own anonymous fourteenth-century words:
'Therefore swink and sweat in all thou canst
and may'st, to get thyself a true knowing and
feeling of thyself as thou art.'

So get swinking immediately.

 BUILDERS DO IT BY THE SEA

Bill is a builder and a mystic.
And it happens in Southend.
He doesn't live there.
But legs it down there when he can.
Because he loves to contemplate the sea.
Gaze on it with love and fascination.

You're having a laugh, aren't you?
Bill? I mean, I've known him since he was so high!
Know everything there is to know about Bill, I do!

Everything, yes.
Except that which matters most to him.

 ORGASM

When the orgasm strikes,
it is almost as if it is done to you.
It has a will of its own,
and can't be called back.
You can live it, experience it, enjoy it –
but you can't control it.
Amidst the gasp we can only
submit and let it flow.

Infusion. The word mystics use to
describe an experience of
God, a union with God, so intense
that we are taken over by it,
however momentarily. It is as though
it is done to us.

Experience shows that both orgasm and infusion
are more likely beyond the confines of
synagogue, mosque or church.

 LONELY

Not an unusual story, but a sad one nevertheless.
Mike despaired of his loneliness.
Not this lonely, he begged. Not always. *Please.*

He'd experienced the love of God.
And it was beautiful. But it wasn't enough.
He wanted someone he could touch. Was this wrong?

No.

Mysticism is as much about human friendship
as it is about God.
The small group of women who followed,
supported and cared for Jesus – even
to the cross and beyond – were as much part of his reality
as his Father in heaven.

Not to mention the disciple he particularly loved – John.

Friendship.

COULD YOU BE QUIET, PLEASE?

Sometimes there must be silence.
Not just a bit of momentary quiet, though that's a start.
But silence.

Because sometimes life is so unutterably bleak;
the situation so difficult;
the darkness so heavy;
the pain so pressing and pointless;
the outcomes so wretched;
that we reach a place beyond words.
Silence.
Words are not the currency here.
They have no value.

Just silence.
The big ache.
The desolation.
Wilderness.
Silence.
And God?

 NOTHING MINOR

There is an arrow aimed at your heart.
It's coming straight for you.
No time to move.

What?!

It's OK, though.
The arrow – it's from God.

Phew! That's a relief!
I was worried for a moment.

No need.
You can relax.
It's only going to kill you.
Nothing minor.

Kill me?
But I was quite fond of life in a strange sort of way.

Sorry. Did I misunderstand?
I thought you wanted to grow.

A PRESENT? FOR ME??

On Margaret Potter's memorial
stone in Ross-on-Wye, are the following words:
'All the way to heaven is heaven.'

Next to it, on the memorial stone
of Dennis Potter, is written this:
'And all of it a kiss.'

All the way to heaven is heaven.
And all of it a kiss.

The present is the only opportunity for union
with God which we have.
The divine moment is now.
Pray from your present – painful, blissful, hilarious, dull.
Pray from what you are.

And you may feel the kiss.

 THE CRADLE OF FILTH

Union costs.
Check out the cradle of filth.
It's evidence.

*(Some people are pleased to call the cradle of filth
a 'manger',
but I've never seen or smelt a clean stable,
so for me it remains a cradle of filth.)*

Someone strikes out at you in some way.
You react with attack or defence. Fine.
It's meant you've survived.
But beyond survival, which is an OK ambition,
is love, which is a grand ambition.

Trouble is, love will ask you to be vulnerable.
Love will ask you to receive the strike, not react to it.
Difficult when you're feeling threatened. Very.

But then like Jesus, we have to start somewhere.
He started in a cradle of filth. Union costs.
Being vulnerable has *never* felt good.

HOW WILL I KNOW?

You know you have reached the kebab shop
by the sweet aroma.
You know you're home when you feel your
key turn inside the front door.
And you know you are in a state of some health
when your three defining characteristics are
tranquillity, gentleness and strength;
when your actions are peaceful, gentle and strong.

Thus, to be 'fussy, unstable, anxious, pessimistic,
worried, intolerant or wobbly' are
signs of ill-health; symptoms of the self-made,
self-acting soul.

Such at least was the diagnosis of St John
of the Cross. Thank you, Doctor.

Now for the kebab. Then home.

WHEN?

When did you notice the bars?

When did you feel for the first time
the absence of freedom?
Trapped. Limited. Boundaries.
The slamming door and you're inside.
The airless room with no windows to open.
The closed circle with no way out.

Lines thou shalt not cross.
Rules thou shalt not break.
Things thou shalt not have.
No. Can't. Don't. Never.

When did you first notice the fact that you aren't free?

Yet still . . . this life . . . penetrated . . .
penetrated by eternity.
Crazy dream.
This prison – penetrated by eternity . . .

THE FORBIDDEN WORD

Sex. What's it about?
Whether it's with yourself or with someone else,
it could be about many things.
Lust, loneliness or longing?
A mix of these?
Creation?
Love?

Mystics, however, hesitate with that word.
Just as actors don't like mentioning
the, er, *Scottish play*, mystics hesitate with love.
For their journey increasingly reveals the
scarcity of it within themselves.

Love. It's a four-letter word and God swears by it.
But for mystics, it's like Macbeth. (Oops!)
Rarely mentioned.
Particularly during sex.
For sex, like life, is about many things.

⟨⟩ ABSOLUTELY AWE-FULL ⟨⟩

Tell me about mysticism.

Why?

Because I want to teach it to others.

Then go away.

Go away?

Go away. And come back when you are in awe of others.

✡

Ask self-importance to leave.
(There may be a row.)
And use the new space created within,
the fresh inner emptiness,
as a front room where others can be invited,
respected, contemplated.

Warning: This might lead to feeling awe-full.

WHAT THE BUTLER SAW

The butler had planned well. He
always planned well. He had given the
chef and maid the evening off. The house
was quiet. Just as the master liked it,
when Harriet came to call.
They could relax. Things could happen.
They were alone.

Not quite alone. For the butler remained.
He had told his master he would be visiting an
aunt in Brighton. But his aunt would have to wait.
(Not hard. She didn't exist.)
Instead, he was kneeling down at his
master's door, eye pressed hard against the keyhole.

Don't even ask what the butler saw . . .

And don't ask what the mystic saw either.
That's *their* experience.

Ask rather, what have *I* seen?

HOLD THE FRONT PAGE

Today, you are a newspaper editor.
You have various stories on your desk.
The question is: which one are you going to
lead with? Which one is going to sit
under the heavy headline, and enjoy prominence?

There are many stories in your
reality at the moment. Which one will you
allow to dominate today? Which bit of reality
will you choose to live from? It's a question
mystics will be aware of.

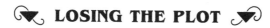 LOSING THE PLOT

The Guru or Messiah comes along
and says that really, very few things matter
at all, but those which do, matter a lot.
The adventure has begun.

Then come the excited followers. They add just
a few things
of their own to the list of things that matter, to
make it slightly more practical – but still keep a
sense of eager purpose.

Then come the pedants, who can quite
see that, long term, unless someone brings
order to this new energy, the whole thing
is going to disintegrate into chaos.
That which once flowed free is now set in stone.
The adventure is over.

It doesn't take long for a religion to lose the plot.
Mystics tend to like the original.

THE ULTIMATE ENEMY

Before she had children, drugs and alcohol
could numb the pain.
After she had children, she decided these paths
were not an option.

So what now? For now there was no way out –
except to binge on cleaning, mass clearouts and the like.
Or not to eat. Or get pregnant again.
Anything to get back in control.
Anything to numb.
Anything is better than to live the sadness.

Or is it?
Is the mystic learning to live the sadness?
Because if you can feel the sadness,
you might just feel the joy too.
Small joy to start with. But freedom often starts small.

For the mystic, the ultimate enemy is not to feel sad.
But to feel numb.

 **I AM**

I am the bubble floating precarious
in the very sharp pin factory.
I am the empty crisp packet tossed
and whisked by the fast wind.
I am the feather caught in the fury
of the big crashing sea.
I am not in control.
But I am loved.

This is the trust written deep in the bones
and marrow of mysticism.
Somehow, a trust – a trust of what is,
a trust of what has been,
and a trust of what shall be.

I am the distant figure, stepping off the cliff,
free falling towards the rocks below . . .

It's OK.

 THE CHANGING TATTOO

I went to the tattooist in Camden, and asked for
a changing tattoo. She said no can do,
a changing tattoo.

I was sad. I so wanted a tattoo.
The trouble is, the colours I like,
and the stories which move, and
the symbols which speak, and the
words which grip, and the pictures which grab me, *now* –
well, they are different from the colours, stories,
symbols, words and pictures of last year.

Life is change.
But a tattoo is permanent.
What else is permanent?
The fact that life is change.

CALL THAT AN EDUCATION?

We are told to work hard at school,
for this, they say, is a rational world:
'Work hard and be in control of your life.
We *are* in control. You *can* have what you want.'

Really?

We are told science has the answer.
We are told the experts, the specialists, are
working on it now.
Some years away from the breakthrough,
but we'll get there.
We *are* in control. You *can* have what you want.

Only we aren't, and we can't.
And the price? Depression.

We have been educated for depression.
We *should* have been prepared for mystery.

IT'S BEYOND BELIEF. FRANKLY.

You hear it again and again from people
you'd previously thought normal.
They speak of an experience of peace or acceptance,
joy, love, presence, light, or belonging –
which releases them into a deep awareness
of unity, oneness, with all that is around.

Some name the experience 'God'. Some don't.
But it is life-staining, life-changing, life-sustaining.
It's irrational. It's beyond belief. It's far out.
Far away. But far away so close.

 THE BOX

Everyone has spiritual experiences,
for everyone is spiritual.

Some people then go on to make
a religion out of these experiences.
Very understandable.
Tidies them up. Puts them in a box.
Instead of saying 'Here are my experiences,'
they say 'Here is my religion.'
All boxed and sorted.

The trouble with boxes, however,
is that they tend to be airless and things inside get stale.
Religions can very easily become boxes,
and places of airless decay.

You are spiritual.
May religion serve you. Not kill you.

# 59 SECONDS WILL DO

The mystic sets aside a time to pray –
for unless there is *one* special time in the day,
there is *no* special time in the day.

The mystic removes his watch when he prays –
just for a moment no slave to time.

The mystic removes her shoes when she prays –
just for a moment the travelling is done.

The mystic sits or kneels comfortable yet alert.
Comfortable, for there is no stillness in restless fidget.
Alert, for this time is not a substitute for sleep.

Palms face upwards,
for this is an encounter with the divine.

A note book and pencil –
to note down distracting thoughts.
You can come back to them later.

Now draw from the well of your experiences
in the last 24 hours. And speak. 59 seconds will do.

 THE GREAT UNWALLING

Tell me about mysticism.

Why?

I am weary of people. I need separation!

Then go away.

Go away?

*Go away. And come back when you are weary
of separation. And need people.*

✡

Truth has to be worked out in relationships with others.
Neighbours, partners, children, enemies, friends,
household pets, vermin, estate agents.
It's part of the great unwalling of the universe.
For others know everything I don't,
and are everything I'm not.

 ON BEING REPULSIVE

It is a serious mistake to make religion
out of our *best* bits; the things you like
about yourself and do rather well.
No. Religion should fearlessly be constructed
out of our *worst* bits; our most
repulsive moments.

Any religion can hold your ideals, your beautiful ideas.
But what of your jealousy, meanness, resentment?
Your tantrums, greed, moodiness, judgements, laziness?
Your self-promotion, self-pity, self-centredness?

Such things, after all, are the stuff of life.
You've come home when you find a religion
which helps you to live hopefully and joyfully
amidst *these* little monsters.

CONCERNING THE SANDWICHES

The small man boarded the royal yacht
gripping tight his little box of sandwiches.
The invitation to the special floating
banquet safe in his pocket.

No taker he, though!
Hence the little box of cheese and pickle,
ham and gherkin.
He'd pay his way, chip in, do his bit.

The young steward had said there was no need, sir.
Everything was laid on, sir, everything was gift.
Huh!! Nonsense. He'd show 'em!

No.
The proper response to love is to accept it.
Receive it.
Put down your little box. Please.

 # BROKEN EGGS

There's no going back.
Ever.
There's no going back ten minutes,
let alone ten years.
Like the omelette, we are what we are,
because we've been through what we've been through.
Unmaking all that is too fiddly even for God.

So no, there's no going back,
no return to the Garden of Eden. It's barred to us.
And so to the next question:
Is there a way forward?
We've discovered God can't unmake omelettes,
but can he give the broken a future?
It's a question worth asking when you next pray . . .

 **UNTIL WE HAVE HEARTS**

Organized religion is a holding operation
until we have hearts;
mysticism is daring to live as though
we have them already.
Organized religion knows we are our own
worst enemies and need protecting from ourselves;
mysticism knows that too –
but suggests that we may
also be our own best friends.
Organized religion knows we can't cope
with too much truth, and so places
walls of difference between us and others;
mysticism knows the walls of disunity
do not reach to heaven.

The friendship between organized religion
and mysticism is sometimes a little strained . . .

BF

Before Freud, who knows what happened?
Before he created the couch, what did people do?

Before Freud said,
'Let there be long and slightly expensive conversations
about your parental hang-ups,'
how did people come to terms with these
rather fundamental matters?

We'll never know.
Although Jesus, in the year 1900 BF,
showed an amazing ability both to be
in close union with his heavenly Father –
and yet remain vividly separate.
His life displayed an ability to argue with his parent,
submit to his parent, listen to his parent,
scream at his parent, talk with his parent,
love his parent.
And not a couch in sight.

BF
JC

THE STRANGEST GIFT

You'll need a pure heart to see God,
said the preacher.
But Mavis didn't have a very pure heart.
She must wash it!

So she scrubbed it with bleach –
but just smelt like a public toilet.
She polished it with furniture wax –
but smelt only like a tired old chair.
She rubbed it with aromatic oils –
but felt only like a cheap jar of pot-pourri.
She'd never see God. Ever.

Tears of frustration flowed.
Salty tears, down her cheeks, down her front,
soaking shirt, soaking through, soaking heart.
Washing heart.

Then God.

Purity wasn't quite what she had imagined.

PS. The preacher hadn't seen God in years.

 JULIAN AND THE NUT

Julian of Norwich took a nut once,
and suddenly, well –
she was all over the place!

It became a universe in itself.
It became the whole of creation!
There, in her hand.

And she knew nothing except that
God made it
God loves it
and God keeps it.
Which for nothing is quite a lot really.

God speaks through the strangest of things
for those who have eyes to see.

Nuts.
Definitely.

 VINCENT

Shortly before he shot himself,
the artist Vincent Van Gogh said that when
he died, he hoped he'd go where the
daring people go.

If such a place exists, he
will be there now with, amongst
others, many mystics.

People who dared to face themselves;
people who dared not to follow the crowd;
people who dared to examine their motives;
people who dared communion with creation;
people who dared contemplation above exploitation.

These are daring paths.
They may be yours.
If so, Vincent awaits you,
in the place where the daring people go.

A CITY SET ON A HILL

Reality is a city set on a hill.
Sometimes so clear on the horizon,
that the detail is stunning.
Sometimes so shrouded in mist,
that we wonder if it's there at all.

Reality is a city set on a hill.
We view it from afar.
And we have mixed feelings.
So strongly pulled towards it.
So strangely frightened by it.

Ultimately, we know it's where life lies.
But to travel there, we must leave the Land
of Fantasy – a land we know well,
and have lived in a long time.
Indeed, sometimes, it seems it's all we have.

Reality is a city set on a hill.
Anyone out there with the guts for the journey?

ORCHESTRAL MANOEUVRES

It was all going very well,
till the conductor suggested the violin be
quiet for a while.
And not just any violin.
The *first* violin!
The first violin be *quiet*?? Unheard of!

If, for the sake of the symphony,
for the sake of the song,
you were asked to put down
your violin for a bit,
while the flute played,
how would you do it?

Would you lay it on your lap with grace?
Or hurl it at the flautist in anger?

You are important.
But don't be self-important.

IF

If I believed in love, imagine the wonder;
If I believed in love, imagine the change.
If I could for one minute
Put aside my hate and fear,
I do believe I could be rearranged.

If I believed in yearning, aching Father;
If I believed in Mother's holding arms;
If I could for one minute
Let that God inside my soul
Receive, amidst the shit and flux, the calm.

If I believed the nail-pinned cry, 'Forgive them,'
The Jesus words 'My peace I give to you.'
If I could for one minute
Open out my ruined soul
And feel the change in all I think and do.

If
If I believed
If I believed in love.

 FATHER TO SON

I said there was no need to cry.
But then I cried first, as we said goodbye
for your first trip away.
By the school gates.
Father and son.

Do you think we might be friends?
One day maybe. Union.
Across the chasm of awkward growth,
failed familiarity and faltering letting go.

I said there was no need to cry,
but I cried first, as we kissed.
By the school gates.
Father and son.

Maybe another Father cried first.
By the heavenly gates.
Two thousand years ago.
His Son's first trip away.

HOW TO HAVE AN AFFAIR

So now we know.
Singles clubs tend to be full of women.
Where are the single men?
Apparently playing with trains, going fishing,
that sort of thing.

Being male can be a triumph of imagination
over relationship.
Being female can be a triumph of relationship
over imagination.
Mystics need *both*.
Imagination to establish our separate and special identity.
Relationship to link us with others.

Utterly separate
AND
gladly relating.

One is an affair of the head.
The other is an affair of the heart.
Together, they become an affair of the soul.

PRACTICAL

A book called *Practical Mysticism* was
published at the outbreak of World War One.
There had been some debate amongst the publishers.
Should they postpone publication, till the destruction and
agony was over? They decided No. If mysticism
couldn't forge a strong spiritual vision which
could 'transcend, hold and enfold the nightmare',
then what was it worth?

Joan of Arc, Florence Nightingale and
General Gordon all knew the stench and wrench of battle.
But they knew also, 'the light that never changes,
above the eye of the soul, above the intelligence'
(St Augustine).

 ABSENCE

When the little boy has been told that
his dad is coming to take him out this Saturday,
it's very hard when his dad doesn't turn up.
His mum can console him, but no consolation
heals the absence, or answers the 'Why?'

If this disappointment is repeated over
a period of time, the pain goes very deep indeed.
As does the pain of people experiencing
the absence of God. One Christian mystic
called it the 'dark night of the soul'.

He wasn't joking.

 OH CHRIST!

Strange to say, Jesus Christ did not come into this
world to be an expletive.
He came into this world to show us what
union looked like, felt like, lived like.

For Christians believe that Jesus embodied union
with both God and people, heaven and earth;
that he held within himself a remarkable intimacy
with both the beyond and the here and now;
with both the perfect and the less than perfect.
Which did he love more?
It would be very hard to say.

No wonder Christian mystics gather round
Jesus, like bees gather round the fat flower,
and art critics, round a newly discovered Rembrandt.
Jesus Christ! Indeed . . .

MINDERS. KEEPERS.

Is there anyone looking out for you?
It's quite important because mystics can sometimes
feel that they're going a little mad.
And to have someone who they can
refer to occasionally, talk with in confidence –
well, it makes a big difference.

They don't need to be a great saint.
(There aren't any anyway.)
Just a person you trust, and who has explored a little
further than you in matters of the soul.

Anyone come to mind?

Mystics need minders.

THE STUPID WOMAN

She couldn't tell you who the singer is.
She doesn't know who wrote the song.
And as for which album it's on . . .

Hopeless.

She doesn't know who wrote the book.
Or what it might be called.
(Although she might be able to tell you
what colour it is. Huh!)

And could she give you chapter and verse
from Holy Scripture? Fat chance, frankly.
She knows nothing, that woman.

Except . . .
she knows when a song moves her.
And when a book speaks.
And when Holy Scripture burns with meaning.

So she knows everything that matters.
Wish I was stupid like her.

 YURI AND THE PRIEST

When Yuri Gagarin returned to earth
from space, and reported that he hadn't
seen God, a Russian Orthodox priest
sensibly pointed out that 'if you haven't seen
God on earth, you will never see him in heaven'.

This is true. But God or the beyond,
can't suddenly be conjured up. Like making a fire,
there *is* preparation – but in the end, it is
gift, surprise, and dangerous.

For when the beyond strikes, we are bruised
by wonder, crippled by awe, and humbled by
acceptance. We are left for dead. Feeling
only how good it is to be alive.

 **KNOW CHANGE**

Some people think they just
need to know a bit more. Then everything
will become clear, be explained, sorted.
And they'll be changed.

What a load of tosh. To 'know' changes nothing.
Hitler knew. Stalin knew. All the most evil people in
the world know stacks. They'd probably make a very
good pub quiz team.

What *does* change people is when they
stop exploiting others – and start contemplating
them. Looking at people not as targets to hit,
objects to exploit or problems to solve –
but as mysteries to reflect on.
Wishing the best for them, however
hard it might be.

Now *that*'s what I call change.

 **AWARENESS**

Awareness isn't a very sexy idea.
But it has its uses.
Awareness of traffic on the road, for instance.
That's pretty handy where I live.
And so is an awareness of how I feel
and why I feel it; an awareness of the state I'm in.
That's pretty handy where I live as well.

For it is out
of that state that I will treat others.

Feeling insecure? That's OK. But don't take it out on
the postman.
Feeling happy? That's fine. But don't assume your
neighbour is.

Awareness.

 RELIGION MUST DIE

Religion must die.
It has bound and tied too many
with its moral demands.
Sin-centred,
rule-rampant,
obey or else!
Hear the gaunt-eyed victims scream within,
see the shackle-legged prisoners stagger
amidst this nightmare of control.

Fear.
Guilt.
Squirming like the field mouse
in the clamp-claws of the hawk.

I know Jesus has said it all before,
but we're saying it again:
Religion must die.
The institution is over.
It's time to find God.

A CROSS WITH A VIEW

What you learn on a cross is not
to wriggle too much, not to wrestle.
Because it doesn't help, it doesn't get you free,
and only increases the pain where the
nails are biting.

Instead, you accept it,
and begin to realize that hoisted high,
you at least have a goodish view,
and gathered round are one or two
friends who aren't there just for the jollies.
But for you. Because you matter to them.

You cry, yes. But then sometimes you
find yourself laughing. And believing –
that some day, someone might come and take you down.
Because you're never going to get down by yourself . . .

TENSION

For many Muslims, music is to be avoided
as it excites the senses. But it has always held a
special place amongst the Sufi brotherhoods.
Beating, chanting and dancing are all used
to intensify awareness of God, and to
forget the things around them.
(Which of course is the origin of the
Whirling Dervishes.)

There is a tension for them between the keeping
of the Sharia, the law of Islam, and the
experience of love between God and the
soul. But Sufis traditionally hold to both.

Let all mystics stay close to the ancient signposts,
and the tedious laws. They are antidotes to
fatuous frenzy, and stupid self-importance
of the untethered mystic. . . .

⚒ NO PARTY GAME ⚒

The three prime reasons for suicide in Britain
are alcoholism, depression and social isolation.

Alcoholism – numbing the pain.
Depression – being denied what you desire.
Social isolation – failure in finding a place to belong.

Mysticism means a journey towards the pain.
Mysticism means facing up to the denied desires.
Mysticism means risking relationships.

Mysticism isn't a party game.
It can be the difference between life and death.

THE DEVIL'S MYSTICS

Every generation has these.
People who's main joy is to
contemplate their own navel.
The trouble is, their navel, though highly
absorbing for them, is a very small
piece of reality. Consequently, the smell
left in the room when they've left,
is one of huge self-indulgence.

If mysticism doesn't strengthen you for love,
forget it.
For mystics and non-mystics, same rules apply:

By their fruits you will know them.

 GROWING UP

When he was small, the boy's room
was filled with a thousand different
bits, gadgets, discoveries, toys, coins,
stickers, figures, models, drawings, comics. The little
shelves heaved with a million glorious distractions.

As he grew up, his interests focused, and
he gradually said a releasing No to the
millions, and a deepening Yes to the few.

Jesus said 'Seek first the Kingdom of God.'
From multiplicity to simplicity, from distraction
to focus. Whatever else it's about, it's
about growing up.

BITTER SWEET

Sweet mystery who loves my jagged edges,
Sweet mystery who hugs my broken glass,
Sweet hope holds close my shattered painful pieces,
Sweet mystery beyond my human grasp.

Sweet mystery so close amidst my crying,
Sweet mystery who hears my asking soul,
Sweet hope which like my heart keeps quietly beating,
Sweet mystery, sore wounded, wounds enfold.

Sweet mystery, I've chased you to exhaustion;
Sweet mystery, I've sought to pin you down;
Sweet hope, you've been evasive to my searchings;
Sweet mystery, now I'm waiting to be found.

 AN APOLOGY

It was not an apology I was expecting.
God saying sorry.
To me.

For I'd always been told it should
be the other way round.
Me saying sorry.
To God.

But it wasn't like that.
This time, it was God saying sorry to me,
God on his knees.
'After all that you've been through,
I will make it up to you.
And I'm sorry.'

I didn't know where to put myself.

PRAYER OF GENTLENESS

Like the touch of a butterfly on my skin,
I feel your heart touch mine.
As I peer, like an innocent child, round
the edge of the curtain,
I see your beauty.
With bowed head, and shaded eyes,
I behold your glory.
In warmth and safety, I feel your presence.
Through loving and being loved,
I live your existence.
In gentleness, I find your forgiveness,
your guidance, your love.
I thank you.
(Simon Lord)

 **TECHNIQUE**

So you've read the little self-help book.
You've been to the evening class on how to do it.
You've bought the manual,
listened to the expert,
sat in on the group discussion,
seen the video and studied the accompanying booklet.
You've checked out the website.
You've probably got the amusing T-shirt too.

In short, you've learnt the technique.
Such life skills! Marvellous.

So all you need now is to be born again.
And again.
And, er, again probably.

And then again.

Beyond, beneath and above technique –
is the birth-giving Spirit of God.

TRUE

Tea for two,
just God and you
don't mind if I do,
if it's true.
True about true love.

True love does not say 'I love you,
so be what I want you to be,'
True love says 'I love you and wish you well,
even if that "well" does not include me.'

Tea for two,
just God and you.
In love.

But if God's not invited,
and it's tea for one with you in a tantrum –
he doesn't shun.
Because it's true what they say about love.

True.
Phew!
God wishes you well.
Well, well, well.

STARS IN THEIR SIGHS

It's not that the Bible is down on astrology.
In fact, some rather famous astrologers
brought gold, frankincense and myrrh
to the baby Jesus – and thus gained a
nativity play immortality
they may be something less than ecstatic over.

The trouble is, though, the stars don't know your name.
They are matter. And you don't matter. Frankly.
For all their magnificence and majesty, they can't
actually rustle up a heart between them.

God *does* know your name, however.
Or rather, like a child longing for the seaside,
he is waiting for you to speak it.
Waiting for you to tell him.

Huh! The games lovers play . . .

THE ROVERS RETURN

The soul is a pub jointly owned
by four very different characters.
Affection, Sensuality, Reason and Imagination.
What a merry partnership!
Enough to drive you from drink . . .

Affection reaching out in love.
Sensuality feeling the peach-soft pleasures.
Reason, cool-eyed, discerning truth and crap.
Imagination exploring dark and light.

In truth, The Rovers Return was like
a second home. Best of course when all four
partners were around.

The place had soul. The place *was* soul.
Yours.

Opening times? Up to you really . . .

THE ABC OF GOD

The ABC, the 1–2–3,
Both he and she,
Inviting me –
It's the Trinity!

You don't know nothing,
If you don't know that.
You're a cardboard cut-out,
You're a dunce's hat.

It's the ABC, the FSS,
Father Son and Spirit
And the answer's Yes.

So say she's a mystery
Say he's a clown
But when God lives inside you
It's a party hitting town.

That's the ABC,
Dum diddle dum dee
'Cos it's all been said
To Daisy and Fred.

*(Little-known playground chant of fourteenth-century mystics,
showing early explorations into God as community.)*

 A BLESSING OF SORTS

May now the armies within, which struggle,
begin to make peace.
Face the fears which so fill, which cripple
and kill, make them foolish.
May anxiety know, it's the end of the show,
it is over.
May the longings which ask, which knock,
now bask in God's smile.
May life's limits which stress, frustrate and depress,
hear an answer.
And may your name on God's heart, be the start,
of all ventures ahead.

EPILOGUE

Perhaps when it's all over
And the impossible is true
And my desperate fear of living
Has finally left the room

Yes perhaps when it's all over
And there's none to do us harm
We'll see the past for what it is
The storm before the calm

Yes perhaps when it's all over
And the fire burns in the hearth
And peace and right and justice
Have come to make us laugh

Yes perhaps when it's all over
And there's no cause for alarm
We'll see the past for what it is
The storm before the calm